RELATIVITY : THE ARCHITECTURE OF REALITY

AF798364

MANAAHIL AMIN

Copyright © Manaahil Amin
All Rights Reserved.

This book has been self-published with all reasonable efforts taken to make the material error-free by the author. No part of this book shall be used, reproduced in any manner whatsoever without written permission from the author, except in the case of brief quotations embodied in critical articles and reviews.

The Author of this book is solely responsible and liable for its content including but not limited to the views, representations, descriptions, statements, information, opinions and references ["Content"]. The Content of this book shall not constitute or be construed or deemed to reflect the opinion or expression of the Publisher or Editor. Neither the Publisher nor Editor endorse or approve the Content of this book or guarantee the reliability, accuracy or completeness of the Content published herein and do not make any representations or warranties of any kind, express or implied, including but not limited to the implied warranties of merchantability, fitness for a particular purpose. The Publisher and Editor shall not be liable whatsoever for any errors, omissions, whether such errors or omissions result from negligence, accident, or any other cause or claims for loss or damages of any kind, including without limitation, indirect or consequential loss or damage arising out of use, inability to use, or about the reliability, accuracy or sufficiency of the information contained in this book.

Made with ♥ on the Notion Press Platform
www.notionpress.com

To every soul who has ever looked up at the night sky and felt curiosity rise like a quiet spark — this is for you.

For the dreamers who chase starlight,

for the minds enchanted by physics,

and for the hearts that believe science is a kind of magic.

May these pages remind you that the universe is not only to be studied,

but felt... wondered... and loved.

Contents

Foreword

This book invites you into a world where science becomes a language of wonder and curiosity becomes a compass to the universe. Through clear ideas and gentle imagination, it explores space, time, and the elegant laws that shape reality. You do not need to be a physicist to walk these pages — only a heart open to learning and a mind willing to look up and ask why.

As you read, may you find beauty in equations, poetry in the stars, and comfort in knowing that the universe is far more magical and meaningful than it first appears. Let this be a quiet beginning to your journey into relativity — not just as a topic, but as a way of thinking, questioning, and dreaming. The cosmos is wide, and curiosity is the first step toward understanding it.

Preface

This book began as a quiet curiosity — a question about how the universe moves, breathes, and holds its secrets in the folds of space and time. What started as fascination soon became a journey through ideas that changed not only science, but the way we see ourselves in the cosmos. Relativity is not just theory; it is perspective — a reminder that reality bends, time stretches, and truth is often more beautiful than imagination.

I wrote these pages not as a physicist sharing facts, but as a learner sharing wonder. Each chapter was shaped with the hope that anyone, regardless of background, could feel the elegance of physics and the poetry hidden within equations. If this book makes one reader pause, look at the sky, and feel both small and infinite at once — then its purpose is fulfilled.

This work is a tribute to curiosity, patience, and the belief that science belongs to all who dare to question. May these thoughts guide you gently through the universe — and may they inspire you to explore beyond it.

Acknowledgements

To my family, who shaped my world long before I studied the universe — thank you for filling my childhood with curiosity, wonder, and unwavering support. Your belief in me has always been the foundation on which my dreams stand. To my friends, who shared long conversations, late-night questions, and laughter through every phase of this journey, I am endlessly grateful. You kept my mind open and my heart grounded.

My deepest appreciation extends to my teachers and mentors, who first introduced me to the became poetry, and the cosmos transformed from a distant mystery into a world I longed to explore. Thank you for nurturing my fascination with science and encouraging me to chase questions larger than life.

And to someone very special — the quiet force who inspired this journey in ways words can only hint at. You are the one who nudged my thoughts toward relativity, who made the universe feel both vast and personal. Through countless discussions, gentle challenges, and unspoken encouragement, you turned curiosity into purpose. This book carries the imprint of those moments, those questions, and that constant presence that pushed me to think deeper and reach higher. You believed in the idea when it was only a spark, and your faith helped turn it into light.

Finally, I express my gratitude to the authors, physicists, researchers, websites, and scientific works that illuminated my path. From timeless texts to trusted online archives and modern science platforms, each source helped refine understanding, deepen perspective, and bring clarity to complexity. This work stands on the shoulders of the brilliant minds and reliable resources that came before it.

And to every dreamer who has ever looked up at the night sky and wondered — may these pages remind you that the universe is not only to be observed, but felt, questioned, and understood. Curiosity is the first step toward discovering infinity.

Prologue

Before equations were written and theories were named, there was simply wonder — a human gaze lifted toward the sky, searching for meaning in the quiet glow of stars. Science began not in laboratories, but in hearts that refused to stop asking why.

This book follows that same spirit. It is not only about space and time, but about curiosity — the force that bends thought the way gravity bends light. As you turn these pages, may you travel not only through the universe, but deeper into your own sense of wonder. For every great discovery begins the same way: with a question, a spark, and the courage to follow it.

CHAPTER ONE

THE PRE-EINSTEIN UNIVERSE

1.1 The Grand Clockwork of Newton

For centuries, humanity gazed at the heavens and believed it understood their rhythm. The planets traced predictable paths, the stars held their places, and the laws of nature seemed fixed and eternal. Isaac Newton had built a universe that functioned like a grand machine — perfectly ordered, precise, and absolute.

In Newton's cosmos, space stretched infinitely in all directions, a vast and unmoving stage upon which the drama of matter unfolded. Time ticked forward uniformly — the same for every observer, the same for the Sun as for a falling apple. Every event had its place in this grand clockwork, governed by laws so elegant that they appeared divine in their certainty.

For nearly two centuries, this picture satisfied the scientific world. Newton's laws described the motions of planets with breathtaking accuracy; they explained tides, projectiles, and pendulums. The universe was seen as a predictable mechanism, and its reliability gave humanity comfort. Space and time were like invisible containers — separate entities, unchanging, unaffected by motion or matter. If one could know the position and velocity of every particle in the universe, Newton suggested, one could predict the future with perfect precision.

Reality seemed deterministic, mechanical, and eternal. But even the strongest foundations can tremble when a single question lingers unanswered.

"What if space and time themselves were not what they seem?"

1.2 A Clockwork Cosmos

For nearly two centuries after Isaac Newton, the universe seemed a grand, precise machine. In this Newtonian picture space stretched infinitely as a fixed, unchanging stage, and time "flow[ed] equably without relation to anything external". In other words, space and time were absolute: the same for all observers. Given Newton's laws, knowing the positions and velocities of all bodies would, in principle, let one calculate the entire future of the cosmos. (As Pierre-Simon Laplace famously phrased it in 1814, an intellect knowing all forces and particle states "would embrace in a single formula" the movements of every atom, making the future as determinate as the past.) Newton's mechanics did indeed account for planets, tides, and projectiles with breathtaking precision. The consistency of these predictions – from Galileo's falling bodies to Halley's comet – gave humanity the comfort of a clockwork universe.

Yet this perfect edifice rested on one deep assumption: that time and space were immutable and independent. Newton's Principia (1687) explicitly defined absolute time and absolute space as real entities: time ticks on "of itself, and from its own nature, without relation to anything external," and space "remains always similar and immovable". In this framework, time would be like a universal metronome and space like a vast, unmoving grid. It was hard for 19th-century minds to imagine otherwise. If time flowed differently for one person than for another, how could clocks agree? If distance changed with motion, how could rulers measure consistently? These questions seemed unthinkable. As a result, the Newtonian world was seen as deterministic and eternal – every event locked into a grand cosmic clockwork.

But the slightest unaccounted detail was cause for alarm in this exacting paradigm. By the late 1800s, cracks were beginning to appear. One crack came not from distant stars but from the behavior of light itself. Around 1800, Thomas Young's famous double-slit experiments confirmed that light behaved as a wave, not as particles. Like waves on water, light waves must travel through something. Physicists thus hypothesized an invisible, all-pervasive medium – the luminiferous ether – filling every corner of space. This ether would play the role that air plays for sound: light waves would "ripple" through it. To work, the ether had to be extraordinarily strange: completely transparent, weightless, frictionless, and filling both empty space and solid matter. It was the ultimate substratum – an absolute frame in which all motion could be referenced. Many scientists took it for granted. "While every effort [was] made to follow citation style rules," one encyclopedia notes, the ether was a **theoretical universal substance believed during the 19th century to act as the medium for electromagnetic waves (light)**.

Into this world of waves and ether came James Clerk Maxwell. In 1865 Maxwell unified electricity and magnetism into a single theoretical framework. His famous equations implied that electromagnetic disturbances propagate as waves. Critically, the mathematics predicted that these waves move at a fixed speed in vacuum – about 300,000 kilometers per second. In fact, Maxwell showed that this speed matched the measured speed of light, leading him to conclude that light is an electromagnetic wave. But fixed relative to what? Newton's laws said velocities add: riding on a train moving at half the speed of light, a bow-spun bullet shot forward should appear to go 1.5 times faster than light would to someone on the ground. Maxwell's theory implied something radically different: no matter how fast the source or observer moves, light should still rush along at c = 300,000 km/s. It was a profound clash. If both the emitter and observer are moving, Newtonian addition would suggest a change in speed, yet Maxwell's wave equations predict a constant c for everyone.

Could both theories be right? Or was something fundamental being misunderstood? By the 1880s, physicists were uneasy. Two great pillars of physics — the mechanical clockwork of Newton and the electromagnetic field of Maxwell — appeared to disagree about the meaning of motion. Space and time, the sacred absolutes of the older view, were beginning to look uncertain. Was the ether really the invisible reference frame? If light's speed never varies, what plays the role of absolute space? These questions hung in the air like a silent challenge to nineteenth-century intuition.

1.3 Light's Mysterious Medium

Scientists began looking for direct evidence of the ether. If Earth were rushing through this cosmic fluid, then light's speed should vary slightly when measured in different directions, much like how wind changes the sound of a whistle if you run toward or away from it. In 1887, Albert A. Michelson and Edward W. Morley devised an ingenious experiment to test this. Michelson, an experimental physicist, had invented an optical interferometer – a device capable of detecting exceedingly small differences in the travel time of light beams.

The setup was deceptively simple in principle. A single light source was directed onto a half-silvered mirror (a beamsplitter), which divided the beam into two perpendicular paths. Each beam bounced off a mirror and returned to recombine at the splitter. If one beam had traveled slightly faster than the other, the recombined beams would exhibit an interference pattern: light and dark fringes whose precise position would shift with any difference in travel time. By carefully rotating the whole apparatus, Michelson and Morley could sample all orientations relative to Earth's motion through space. To eliminate vibrations, Morley mounted the giant interferometer on a thick sandstone slab floating on a pool of mercury, allowing it to rotate smoothly through 360 degrees.

With this powerful tool, the two physicists peered for the slightest "ether wind." They ran their measurements over many nights in the basement of a Cleveland laboratory from spring into summer 1887. They fully expected to see a tiny fringe shift when the light paths were aligned with Earth's motion (speeding up or slowing down one beam). The sensitivity was extraordinary – capable of detecting changes in the speed of light of just a few parts in a million.

Yet no shift appeared. The interference pattern remained unchanged regardless of the apparatus orientation. In every trial, the speed of light came out the same in all directions. "The experiment again failed to detect any motion of the expected magnitude," reported Michelson and Morley. In short, the Earth seemed to be at rest in the ether, or the ether did not exist at all. This null result was astonishing: it was as if nature refused to reveal an absolute frame.

The Michelson–Morley experiment dealt a serious blow to the ether hypothesis. A contemporary encyclopedia notes that by 1887 "the theory [of ether] was seriously weakened... which showed that there was no such effect" of ether drift. The negative outcome was deeply unsettling. It suggested that light behaves as though there is no preferred background at all – a fact utterly at odds with everyday intuition. In response, some physicists proposed mathematical fixes. George FitzGerald and Hendrik Lorentz independently suggested that objects physically contract along the direction of motion through the ether – just enough so that the expected fringe shifts would vanish in the experiment. But this Lorentz–FitzGerald contraction was a curious patchwork: it saved the result of Michelson–Morley at the cost of introducing an ad hoc effect with no underlying explanation. It felt like covering a crack in the wall with another, equally mysterious layer.

1.4 Cracks in the Edifice

In the wake of the null result, physicists stood on unsettled ground. Michelson and Morley's findings implied that no matter how we move, light's speed stays constant. But Newtonian mechanics insisted otherwise. This contradiction gnawed at the foundations. If light's speed is universal, then the simple rules of adding velocities must fail. It meant the old notions of time and space might not be absolute after all. Even Lorentz's contraction, while ingenious, offered no satisfying insight into why rulers should shrink or clocks slow when moving. Scientists felt they were juggling two incompatible pictures of reality.

At the same time, a very different anomaly emerged from the heavens. Astronomers tracking planetary orbits with unprecedented precision discovered that Mercury's orbit did not fit Newton's laws exactly. According to Newtonian gravity, the elliptical orbit of Mercury should precess – its closest point to the Sun (perihelion) should advance – due to the pull of the other planets and the bulge of the Sun itself. The observed rate of this advance was about 5,600 arcseconds per century, mostly accounted for by known effects. But when all these influences were carefully calculated and subtracted, there remained a stubborn leftover of about 43 arcseconds per century. In 1859 French astronomer Urbain Le Verrier first pointed out this "anomalous" precession. (Canadian-American astronomer Simon Newcomb later refined Le Verrier's numbers to 42.98″ by 1882.) No matter how hard they checked Newtonian physics simply could not explain that extra 43″. It was a tiny discrepancy – just a hair's-breadth over a century – but for precision science it was glaring. This orbital puzzle hinted that perhaps gravity's law was incomplete.

Thus by the end of the 19th century, classical physics had its share of disquieting clues. The pillars were still up – Newton's equations still worked for most situations, Maxwell's laws still described electricity and magnetism perfectly – but their relationship was uneasy. How could two halves of physics describe the same universe yet disagree about something as fundamental as motion? Space and time, once thought immutable, suddenly seemed fragile concepts. Could time flow differently for different observers? Could distances really shrink simply because of motion? These questions felt absurd under the Newtonian mindset. As one observer remarked after Michelson's result, the idea that "the speed of light is the same for all observers" was utterly incompatible with Newtonian relativity. Yet experiment after experiment – Michelson–Morley on light, and even careful astronomy on planets – was chipping away at the old order.

And so, as the 1800s turned into the 1900s, physics stood at a crossroads. By the eve of the new century, the stage was set for a revolution. Into this unsettled world stepped a young Swiss patent clerk named Albert Einstein. He was not blinded by tradition; he toyed with "what if" questions. He later recalled wondering *"what it would be like to ride alongside a beam of light (time appears to stop)"* – a simple thought experiment that no physicist before him had given serious weight. The old absolutes of space and time were about to be thrown into doubt. But that story belongs to the next chapter. Physicists of 1900 could only know that their long-held certainties were crumbling, and that a bold new idea would soon be needed to replace them.

1.5 The Moment Before the Revolution

At the dawn of the twentieth century, physics stood on the brink of transformation. The old order of absolute space and time was beginning to fracture — not just through experiment, but through pure thought. The contradictions between Newton's absolutes, Maxwell's light, and the failed ether were not mere curiosities. They were the signs of a deeper truth waiting to be uncovered.

In 1905, Einstein published his paper on what we now call Special Relativity, fundamentally altering our understanding of space, time, and energy. The stage was set for the next great leap: General Relativity — a theory that would reveal gravity not as a force but as the curvature of space-time by mass and energy.

The world of absolute space and absolute time was nearing its end — not with a thunderous collapse, but with a quiet, elegant idea that would change everything. The contradictions of ether, light, and Mercury's orbit were not errors — they were clues. The universe was waiting to reveal its symmetry: a world where the speed of light is constant, and where time itself can stretch, twist, and bend

CHAPTER TWO

Einstein's Leap: The Birth of Special Relativity

2.1 A Question That Changed Everything

The year was 1905 — a year physicists would later call annus mirabilis, the "miraculous year." In a small, dimly lit room of the Swiss Federal Institute of Intellectual Property in Bern, a 26-year-old clerk named Albert Einstein sat surrounded by stacks of technical documents. Day after day, he examined patent applications for electromagnetic devices and machinery, his mind quietly simmering with questions that stretched far beyond the papers before him.

He had no laboratory, no assistants, no prestigious university position. But he possessed something far rarer — a mind unafraid to imagine, to question, and to doubt what others took for granted.

Einstein could not stop thinking about light. Since his teenage years, the puzzle of its constancy had haunted him. He once recalled, "If I pursue a beam of light with the velocity , I should observe such a beam of light as an electromagnetic field at rest." But Maxwell's equations forbade this. Light had no rest frame; it always moved at the same speed, no matter the observer. The paradox gnawed at him. How could nature make such an exception?

Others were busy patching old theories. But Einstein suspected the problem wasn't with light — it was with space and time themselves. What if Newton's absolutes were not fixed after all? What if space and time were woven together, stretching and twisting with motion?

In June 1905, Einstein published a paper titled "On the Electrodynamics of Moving Bodies." It was only 30 pages long — deceptively modest — yet it shattered centuries of thought.

In it, Einstein proposed two simple, daring postulates:

1. The laws of physics are the same in all inertial frames of reference.

Whether you are on a smoothly moving train or standing still on the ground, no experiment can reveal absolute motion.

2. The speed of light in a vacuum is constant for all observers, regardless of their relative motion.

Whether the source moves toward you or away from you, light always travels at kilometers per second.

"The velocity of light... plays a fundamental role, a limit not to be surpassed." — Albert Einstein

From these two statements, Einstein redrew the architecture of reality. If light's speed is always the same, something else must adjust to preserve that constancy. That "something" turned out to be space and time themselves

2.2 Time, Space, and the Collapse of Absolutes

Imagine two observers — one standing still, the other on a train rushing past at half the speed of light. Each shines a flashlight. According to Einstein, both observers will measure the light's speed as exactly the same, even though they are moving relative to each other.

The only way this can be true is if time and space stretch and shrink depending on motion. Time slows down. Lengths contract. What once seemed absolute becomes relative.

This leads to one of the most remarkable consequences: time dilation.

Time doesn't flow the same for everyone. A moving clock ticks more slowly than a stationary one. The faster you move, the more slowly time passes for you relative to someone at rest. This isn't a trick of perception — it's the geometry of reality.

A companion to time dilation is length contraction: moving objects appear shorter along the direction of motion. To an observer watching a spaceship hurtle past at near-light speed, its length seems compressed. But to the astronaut inside, nothing has changed. Both perceptions are correct — each within its own frame of reference.

Another profound implication is the relativity of simultaneity. Two events occurring at the same time for one observer may not be simultaneous for another. Imagine a train moving swiftly through a station. Lightning strikes both ends of the train at the same instant — according to someone standing on the platform. But to a passenger in the middle of the train, the strike at the front reaches them first. For them, time itself has reordered events. Simultaneity has become subjective.

"The distinction between past, present, and future is only a stubbornly persistent illusion." — Albert Einstein

This was no small adjustment to science. It was the collapse of Newton's absolutes — the realization that there is no single, universal perspective. Reality depends on where you are and how you move.

2.3 Energy and Mass: Two Sides of the Same Coin

Then came the most elegant realization of all: energy and mass are not distinct entities. They are two forms of the same essence.

Later in 1905, Einstein published a short follow-up paper containing a deceptively simple equation:

"$E = mc^2$"

This single line changed human understanding forever.

It revealed that even a small amount of matter contains an enormous amount of energy, because the speed of light squared is a colossal number. The energy that powers the Sun, the energy released in nuclear reactions — all trace their roots to this unity of mass and energy. Matter, it turned out, was frozen energy; energy, liberated matter.

The impact of this discovery was immense. Yet Einstein himself was serene about it. He saw beauty more than power in the relationship. To him, it was harmony — a sign that nature's laws are not chaotic, but deeply interconnected.

2.4 Why It Was "Special"

Why "special" relativity? The name reflects the act that this theory applies only to special cases — those involving observers moving at constant speeds in straight lines (inertial frames). It does not describe acceleration or gravity. For that, a deeper theory would be needed.

Even so, this "special" case was revolutionary. It dissolved the very notion of absolute rest. There was no single, privileged viewpoint from which to describe the universe. All motion was relative, and only the relationships between observers had meaning.

Einstein's work did more than solve the puzzle of light. It changed the way humanity thought about reality itself. The universe was no longer a stage of fixed space and steady time. It was a living fabric, where measurements of distance and duration intertwined. Space and time, once thought separate, became a single four-dimensional continuum: spacetime.

CHAPTER THREE

THE NATURE OF SPACE AND TIME

3.1 A Universe Woven Together

By the time Albert Einstein's special theory of relativity began to settle into the scientific world, one truth had become inescapable: the universe was far stranger than human senses had ever suggested. What had once seemed like two distinct entities — space and time — were no longer independent. They were woven together into a single, inseparable fabric: spacetime.

The first person to fully articulate this profound union wasn't Einstein himself, but the German mathematician Hermann Minkowski, one of Einstein's former teachers. In 1908, Minkowski stood before an audience of physicists and declared:

"Henceforth space by itself and time by itself fade away into mere shadows, and only a kind of union of the two will preserve an independent reality."

Those words marked a turning point in physics. What Einstein had glimpsed through intuition, Minkowski expressed with geometry. The world was no longer a stage on which events occurred — it was a four-dimensional continuum where events themselves were part of the fabric.

3.2 Coordinates of Reality

To grasp this idea, imagine marking a location in space — say, a point on the floor of your room. You can describe it with three coordinates: length, width, and height. But this description is incomplete without one more coordinate — when the point is occupied.

Every event in the universe needs not just a "where" but also a "when." A lightning strike, a spoken word, a heartbeat — each occupies a unique position in both space and time. These four coordinates (three of space and one of time) together define an event in spacetime.

In this view, time is not a flowing river that carries events forward. It stands alongside space, forming a grand four-dimensional landscape. The past, present, and future are all points in this continuum. Movement through space alters how we move through time.

The faster an object travels through space, the slower it moves through time. This trade-off isn't poetic metaphor — it's physical law. Every object in the universe moves through spacetime at the same fundamental rate: the speed of light. When you are at rest in space, you're moving entirely through time. When you move through space, you give up some of that journey through time.

This perspective dissolves the comforting illusion of a universal "now." Two observers moving relative to each other slice the spacetime continuum differently. What one calls "the present" may include moments that belong to the other's past or future. The ancient assumption that two events can be simultaneous for everyone loses meaning

In the geometry of spacetime, there is no universal present — only different cross-sections chosen by different observers.

3.3 Worldlines and Light Cones

To visualize the strange geometry, physicists use spacetime diagrams, where time replaces one of the spatial dimensions. On such a diagram, an object's history — its path through time — is called a worldline.

A stationary object traces a straight vertical line upward through time. A moving object tilts its worldline, indicating motion through space as well as time. Light, moving at the ultimate cosmic speed limit, follows a diagonal line. Its path defines the boundary between the possible and the impossible.

These diagonal boundaries are called light cones, and they define the limits of causality. Only events inside your light cone — those close enough that light has had time to reach you — can influence you. Events outside that cone lie beyond reach, forever separated from your experience.

The light cone enforces the universe's most profound rule: cause always precedes effect. Even the most powerful signal cannot leap outside this cone. Doing so would require exceeding the speed of light — something forbidden by the very structure of spacetime itself.

This insight did more than redraw physics; it rewrote our notion of reality itself. Space and time were not absolute arenas, but aspects of a single, malleable geometry. They could stretch, tilt, and warp depending on motion and energy. The true distance between events in this four-dimensional landscape remains constant for all observers — a deep, hidden symmetry underlying the universe.

3.4 The Path Toward Gravity

Einstein himself was initially hesitant about Minkowski's abstraction. He once joked that mathematicians had made his theory "too complicated." But he soon realized this four-dimensional view held the key to his next great challenge: understanding gravity.

If motion through space could affect the flow of time, might not gravity — so closely tied to acceleration — also be a manifestation of spacetime's geometry?

The seeds of this idea were already sprouting in his mind. He began to suspect that gravity was not a mysterious force pulling objects together, as Isaac Newton had imagined, but a result of the curvature of spacetime caused by mass and energy.

The Earth orbits the Sun not because it's tugged by an invisible hand, but because it follows the straightest possible path through curved spacetime — just as a marble rolls along the contours of a stretched rubber sheet.

The implications were enormous. Matter and energy could shape the geometry of the cosmos itself — and that geometry would, in turn, guide how matter moves. The universe was not a stage but an actor in its own story.

By 1911, Einstein was deep in this pursuit. He began to notice subtle effects that special relativity alone could not explain — such as how gravity might influence the passage of time. If motion slowed time, perhaps gravity did too. A clock placed high on a mountain would tick slightly faster than one at sea level, simply because it feels less of Earth's gravitational pull.

This tiny difference, imperceptible in daily life, could one day be measured. And decades later, it was.

Space and time had revealed their unity. They were flexible, relative, and profoundly intertwined. But Einstein wasn't satisfied. His new geometry of motion explained how objects behaved when they moved freely, unaffected by outside forces. What he sought next was a theory that could describe motion when forces — especially gravity — were present.

He wanted to understand not only how time stretched with speed, but how it bent with mass.

To find that answer, Einstein would have to climb higher than ever before — into the very geometry of the cosmos. He would need to rethink gravity itself: not as a force acting through space, but as the bending of space and time. It would take him another decade of struggle. But when it came, it would reveal a universe more elegant and strange than even he had imagined.

CHAPTER FOUR

THE ROAD TO GENERAL RELATIVITY

4.1 The Missing Piece

By 1907, Albert Einstein had already transformed the world's understanding of motion, light, and time. His special theory of relativity described the universe with astonishing elegance — but only for observers moving at constant speeds, within what physicists called inertial frames.

Yet the world was not made of straight lines and uniform motion. Planets traced curved orbits, apples fell to the ground, and every step we took pressed us against Earth's pull. Gravity — the ancient force that had guided Isaac Newton's equations for over two centuries — stood apart from this new elegant geometry of spacetime. Einstein's instinct whispered to him: gravity must be woven into the same fabric.

He began, as always, not with complex mathematics, but with thought experiments — simple ideas born of deep curiosity. One day, sitting at his desk in Bern, a realization struck him that he would later call "the happiest thought of my life."

He imagined a man falling from the roof of a house. During the fall, the man would feel weightless. Objects around him would float beside him, as if gravity had vanished. Within that fleeting frame of free fall, the man would experience the same conditions as an astronaut drifting in deep space.

"A person in free fall experiences no gravity." — Albert Einstein

This moment was no coincidence. It was a clue. Free fall, Einstein realized, is indistinguishable from weightlessness. The same laws of physics that apply in empty space also apply inside a freely falling elevator. Gravity, it seemed, could be transformed away by choosing the right frame of reference.

This led him to a bold principle that would become the cornerstone of his next great theory: the Equivalence Principle.

"A uniform gravitational field is equivalent to a uniformly accelerated frame of reference."

4.2 Acceleration and Gravity: Two Sides of One Coin

In simpler terms, acceleration and gravity are two faces of the same reality.

Imagine being inside a sealed box floating in the emptiness of space. If the box suddenly accelerated upward, you'd feel pressed to the floor — just as if you were standing on Earth. If you dropped a ball, it would fall to the floor in both scenarios.

No experiment inside the box could tell you whether the force you felt came from acceleration or from gravity. This profound insight broke the last chains tying gravity to Newton's vision of a mysterious invisible force.

Einstein realized gravity wasn't acting across space, as Newton imagined. It was a manifestation of the geometry of spacetime itself. Matter doesn't pull on other matter with invisible strings — it tells spacetime how to curve, and curved spacetime tells matter how to move.

4.3 Curvature of Reality

To visualize this, Einstein often turned to a simple image: a rubber sheet. Imagine placing a heavy ball on a stretched rubber membrane. The sheet dips, curving around the ball. Now, roll a smaller marble nearby — it circles the larger ball, not because of an invisible tug, but because the curved surface guides its path.

In the same way, the Sun curves the spacetime around it, and the Earth follows that curvature. It orbits not because it's being "pulled," but because it moves along the straightest possible path in this curved geometry — **a geodesic.**

The idea was breathtakingly beautiful — but turning it into mathematics would demand almost a decade of struggle. Einstein was a physicist of intuition, not a trained geometer. To express his vision, he had to learn the language of tensor calculus and differential geometry from scratch.

During this time, he collaborated with his friend Marcel Grossmann, a mathematician who guided him through the intricate terrain of non-Euclidean geometry. It was an uphill climb through one of the most difficult intellectual landscapes in science.

Einstein's life during these years was one of relentless pursuit. He worked in isolation, often facing skepticism from colleagues. In letters, he confessed that the problem of gravity tortured him — but his conviction never wavered. He believed nature's laws had an inner harmony, and that the same principle of relativity governing motion must govern acceleration and gravity too.

"The years of searching in the dark for a truth that one feels but cannot express... the intense desire and the alternations of confidence and misgiving, until one breaks through to clarity—are only known to him who has himself experienced them."
— Albert Einstein

4.4 Geometry Writes the Law

Gradually, the picture began to emerge. Space and time were no longer static containers; they were dynamic, responsive, alive.

Massive objects like stars and planets distorted the geometry of spacetime around them. A clock placed near a massive body would tick more slowly than one farther away — an effect later named gravitational time dilation. Even beams of starlight passing near the Sun would bend slightly, tracing the curve of space.

These predictions were bold, but they were also testable. Einstein realized that if his theory were correct, astronomers could detect this bending of starlight during a total solar eclipse. Stars near the Sun's edge would appear slightly displaced from their true positions due to the Sun's gravitational curvature.

It would take years before this test could be carried out, but Einstein already sensed he was close to unlocking nature's most profound secret.

By 1915, after nearly a decade of relentless work, he finally completed the equations describing how matter and energy shape spacetime:

$$g_{\{\mu v\}} = \frac{8\pi g}{c^4} t_{\{\mu v\}}$$

On one side of the equation lay geometry, describing spacetime's curvature. On the other side lay matter and energy, the contents of the universe. The two sides were in perfect dialogue.

This was the birth of the General Theory of Relativity, published in November 1915. It replaced Newton's invisible force with a vision of gravity as the geometry of existence. Space and time could now stretch, bend, and ripple. The universe was no longer a passive stage but an active participant in its own unfolding story.

4.5 The Sky Confirms the Theory

When Einstein presented his results to the Prussian Academy of Sciences, he was exhausted but elated. He knew he had rewritten humanity's understanding of the cosmos. But the world at large would not grasp the full significance of his work until four years later, when experiment would finally confirm his predictions.

In 1919, during a total solar eclipse, British astronomer Arthur Eddington led an expedition to measure the bending of starlight. The results matched Einstein's predictions with astonishing precision.

The headlines screamed:

"Revolution in Science! Newtonian Ideas Overthrown!"

Overnight, the quiet patent clerk from Bern became a global icon. Relativity became a household word, and Einstein — a symbol of genius.

But beneath the fame, Einstein remained deeply humble. He often said that his joy lay not in recognition but in the act of discovery itself — the moment when thought aligned with nature's hidden order.

"The most incomprehensible thing about the universe is that it is comprehensible." — Albert Einstein

4.6 A Symphony of Matter and Geometry

With general relativity, Einstein completed the grand unification of motion and gravity. Space and time were no longer rigid containers; they were supple, dynamic, and interconnected. The universe had become a cosmic symphony of matter and geometry — a fabric that could curve, twist, and even ripple.

And indeed, ripple it could. From the heart of his equations came astonishing predictions: gravitational waves — disturbances in spacetime itself, radiating outward when massive objects like stars or black holes collided. Einstein doubted they'd ever be observed, but the mathematics was clear.

Einstein had changed our picture of reality once again. Yet, as always, each answer opened new questions. If spacetime could bend and ripple, could it also expand or contract on cosmic scales? What did relativity say about the universe as a whole — its birth, its shape, its fate?

The next chapter of this story would unfold on the grandest canvas imaginable: the structure and evolution of the cosmos itself.

CHAPTER FIVE

The Fabric of the Cosmos

5.1 A Whisper from the Universe

The year was 1919. The war had ended, and the world — weary and broken — sought new light. Something that reminded humankind of its shared wonder.

And in that year, under the darkened skies of a total solar eclipse, the universe whispered its truth. When Arthur Eddington's photographs revealed that starlight bent ever so slightly as it passed near the Sun, Albert Einstein's equations were confirmed, and reality itself seemed to shift.

The cosmos had curved, and we had measured its curve.

The fabric of the cosmos — space and time woven together — had proven not to be flat, but elastic. Stars, planets, and galaxies pressed into this fabric, sculpting its shape. Light, the purest traveler, followed the geometry, bending gracefully around massive bodies. Time, too, flowed differently in valleys of gravity and on mountain peaks of emptiness.

The universe, once thought to be a rigid clockwork, was revealed to be alive — with rhythm and curvature.

5.2 Space Is Not Empty

To truly grasp this, one must abandon the comforting intuition that space is emptiness. In Einstein's cosmos, space is something — a flexible medium that can stretch, compress, and warp under the influence of mass and energy.

When we say the Earth orbits the Sun, we are really saying that Earth moves along the curved contours of spacetime that the Sun's mass creates.

"The Sun tells spacetime how to curve, and spacetime tells the Earth how to move."

Every object — from a grain of dust to a black hole — leaves its fingerprint upon the geometry of the cosmos. Einstein's equations showed it was not only mass that curves spacetime, but also energy, pressure, and radiation. Every star that shines, every photon that moves, every particle that trembles — all contribute to the architecture of the universe.

The beauty of relativity lies not only in its abstraction but in its measurable manifestations. Subtle ripples that echo through reality. Among these, three stand as its most elegant confirmations:

the bending of light,
the dilation of time,
and the precession of orbits.

5.3 Light, Time, and Orbits

The bending of light, or gravitational lensing, occurs whenever light passes near a massive object. The curvature of spacetime deflects its path, much like glass bends light in a lens.

Distant galaxies, whose light travels billions of years to reach us, often pass near intervening clusters of other galaxies. Their paths distort, so we see multiple images or bright arcs around the cluster.

To the observer, it is as though nature itself has built a colossal cosmic lens — magnifying and reshaping the light of distant worlds. What once was a faint smudge becomes, through gravity's lens, a natural telescope carved by spacetime.

Then comes time dilation, gravity's most subtle trick. Clocks in strong gravitational fields tick more slowly than those in weaker ones. On Earth, the difference is minuscule — nanoseconds between a mountaintop and sea level — but measurable with modern technology.

In orbit, satellites experience weaker gravity, so their clocks tick faster than those on the ground. The designers of the Global Positioning System (GPS) had to incorporate Einstein's corrections, or else every location on Earth would drift by kilometers each day. Every time a phone guides a traveler across a city, it does so by following the rhythms of Einstein's universe.

Even the planets whisper the song of relativity. For centuries, astronomers puzzled over Mercury's orbit. Its closest point to the Sun shifted slightly with each revolution — a few arcseconds per century that Newton's laws couldn't explain. Einstein's general relativity solved it perfectly, predicting the exact precession observed. It was as though the theory had reached back through time and corrected the universe's bookkeeping.

5.4 Black Holes and the Edges of Time

But perhaps the most poetic prediction of all was that of black holes — regions of spacetime so curved that nothing, not even light, can escape their gravity. Though Einstein himself doubted their existence at first, his equations foretold them.

Imagine a star so massive that when its fuel is exhausted, gravity crushes it inward. All paths, all directions, lead inward — a one-way curtain called the event horizon. Beyond it lies singularity, where curvature becomes infinite and the known laws of physics dissolve.

Black holes are not merely cosmic monsters; they are perfect expressions of Einstein's geometry. Around them, time slows nearly to a stop. To a distant observer, an object falling toward a black hole seems to freeze at the edge, its clock ticking slower and slower. But to the falling traveler, the journey continues — toward a fate beyond the reach of any signal.

Yet black holes, for all their darkness, illuminate the depths of relativity. They reveal that gravity is not just a force but a sculptor of time itself. They remind us that space is dynamic and alive, capable of extremes that border on the mystical.

And just as gravity can bend light and slow time, it can also ripple. Einstein predicted that when massive objects accelerate — such as two neutron stars or black holes spiraling together — they send out waves in the fabric of spacetime itself: gravitational waves.

For a century, they remained theoretical, too faint to detect. But in 2015, nearly exactly 100 years after Einstein's prediction, scientists at the Laser Interferometer Gravitational-Wave Observatory (LIGO) heard them — the faint chirp of two black holes colliding over a billion light-years away.

That moment was more than a triumph of science. It was a cosmic echo of Einstein's vision. The universe had spoken in the language of spacetime itself, and humanity had finally learned to listen.

5.5 A Living Universe

These discoveries reshaped not only physics but philosophy. If space and time could bend, ripple, and evolve, then the cosmos itself was not static. Einstein's equations contained a deeper revelation — the universe could expand or contract.

In 1917, seeking stability, Einstein introduced the cosmological constant to keep the universe static. But when Edwin Hubble later observed galaxies receding from us, Einstein realized his equations had always pointed toward an expanding universe. He called the cosmological constant his "greatest blunder" — though it would later return as a symbol of dark energy, the mysterious force driving cosmic acceleration.

Thus, relativity opened the door to cosmology, the study of the universe as a whole. Space was not merely a stage for stars but a dynamic entity that could stretch and grow. Time was not uniform but woven into the evolution of galaxies and the birth of worlds.

The Big Bang itself — the moment when space and time began — was not an explosion in space, but an explosion of space.

Through all this, Einstein's theory has remained the silent architect of our understanding. Every observation of gravitational waves, every image of a black hole's shadow, every map of cosmic expansion — all trace their lineage to his equations.

General relativity does not merely describe the universe; it defines its structure.

Yet, for all its triumphs, the theory is not complete. It does not yet embrace the quantum realm, where uncertainty rules and gravity falters. The dream of uniting relativity with quantum mechanics — a theory of everything — remains the unfinished symphony of modern physics.

Still, Einstein's vision endures, as pure and clear as when he first glimpsed it in his mind's eye:
a universe where space and time dance to the rhythm of mass and energy,
where the cosmos itself is a vast, curved poem written in the language of geometry.

CHAPTER SIX

Cosmic Consequences: From the Big Bang to Black Holes

6.1 A New Language for the Universe

By the time Albert Einstein published his general theory of relativity, he had given the universe a new language — one that spoke of curvature, motion, and the delicate dance between matter and geometry.

Yet even Einstein could not have foreseen how far these ideas would reach. Within a few short years, relativity would escape the confines of falling apples and orbiting planets and stretch across the cosmos itself — to the birth of space and time, the depths of black holes, and the fate of the universe.

The equations of general relativity did not describe a static universe. They allowed — indeed, demanded — a dynamic one.

When Einstein first applied his equations to the entire cosmos, he noticed something astonishing: the universe could not stand still. It would either **expand** or **contract.**

6.2 The Cosmological Constant

To Einstein, this was deeply unsettling. The night sky seemed still. Stars held their fixed positions like silent sentinels. A dynamic universe felt... wrong. To restore balance, he introduced an additional term to his equations: **the cosmological constant**, denoted by Λ .

This constant acted like a subtle outward pressure, a counterweight to gravity, holding the universe in place — a finely tuned equilibrium. It wasn't nature's command but human desire for order. Einstein had, unknowingly, written a patch into the fabric of the cosmos.

"I have created a static universe," he must have thought, "balanced on the knife-edge of Λ."

But the universe had other plans.

6.3 The Expanding Universe

In the 1920s, a Belgian priest and physicist named Georges Lemaître studied Einstein's equations and found that a static universe was mathematically impossible.

He proposed a revolutionary idea: the cosmos is expanding. Space itself is stretching, carrying galaxies away from one another like raisins in a rising loaf of bread. If traced backward, this expansion would converge to a single, incredibly dense point — what he called the "primeval atom" — the seed of what we now know as the Big Bang.

Einstein initially dismissed the idea, reportedly telling Lemaître,

"Your calculations are correct, but your physics is abominable."

But reality soon sided with Lemaître. In 1929, Edwin Hubble, observing distant galaxies through the Mount Wilson Observatory, discovered that their light was redshifted — stretched to longer wavelengths.

The farther away a galaxy was, the faster it was receding. This became known as **Hubble's Law:**

$v = H0d$

Where:

- v = recessional velocity of the galaxy,
- H0 = Hubble constant (rate of expansion),
- d = distance to the galaxy.

The cosmos was not static after all; it was expanding.

6.4 Relativity and the Fate of the Universe

The expansion of space fundamentally changed how scientists understood the cosmos. Relativity had already shown that **spacetime is dynamic**, curving and bending in response to mass and energy. But now it became clear that space itself could **grow**, stretching the very fabric of reality.

Relativity became the **foundation of modern cosmology**, describing not just how gravity works, but how the **universe evolves**. It explained the cosmic microwave background — the faint afterglow of the Big Bang — and predicted that the expansion should slow under gravity's pull.

But in 1998, a new shock awaited physicists. Observations of distant **Type Ia supernovae** revealed that the universe's expansion was not slowing down — it was accelerating.

Some unseen force was pushing galaxies apart faster and faster. In a twist of irony, the very cosmological constant Einstein had once abandoned returned — now reborn as dark energy, a mysterious force that makes up nearly **70% of the universe.**

Even in his supposed "blunder," Einstein had glimpsed the truth.

6.5 Black Holes and Cosmic Horizons

While relativity guided us across the grand scale of the cosmos, it also turned our gaze inward — toward the most terrifying and beautiful objects it could conceive: **Black holes.**

From Einstein's equations, the German physicist Karl Schwarzschild found an exact solution describing spacetime around a perfectly spherical mass. At the center lay a singularity, a point of infinite curvature. Around it existed a boundary where escape became impossible, even for light: **the event horizon.**

For decades, black holes were mathematical curiosities. But as telescopes grew powerful, the universe revealed them everywhere: at the hearts of galaxies, in the remnants of massive stars, and in binary systems where invisible companions devour matter.

Black holes are paradoxes of simplicity and mystery. Defined by only three quantities — mass, charge, and spin — they erase every other detail of the matter that falls into them. Time near their event horizons behaves in ways that defy everyday intuition:

- To an outside observer, time slows.
- Light redshifts to blackness.
- To the falling traveler, time flows normally... until it meets the singularity.

In the 1970s, *Stephen Hawking* extended Einstein's ideas by merging relativity with quantum mechanics. He showed that black holes are not entirely black. Through quantum effects at the horizon, they emit **Hawking radiation** and slowly evaporate over unimaginable timescales. Even in darkness, they whisper the universe's deepest secrets.

In 2019, the Event Horizon Telescope captured the first direct image of a black hole's shadow — a glowing ring of light encircling darkness. It was not just a scientific milestone; it was a portrait of spacetime itself.

Yet black holes also reveal relativity's limits. At their centers, spacetime becomes infinite — a singularity where Einstein's equations break down. Beyond this horizon lies the ultimate goal of physics: to unite general relativity with the quantum laws of particles into a **single theory of quantum gravity.**

Still, even in its incompleteness, general relativity has given humanity a cosmic vision unlike any before. It teaches us that we live in a universe where space stretches, time flows differently in every valley of gravity, and the future of the cosmos is written in the geometry of the present.

The universe may one day slow its expansion and collapse into a fiery end — a "Big Crunch." Or it may continue expanding forever into the cold silence of "heat death." Or perhaps, through quantum fluctuations, new universes may bud and bloom from the fabric of spacetime itself.

Whatever the fate, Einstein's vision remains a guiding light.

He once said:

"I want to know how God created this world. I am not interested in this or that phenomenon. I want to know His thoughts — the rest are details."

From the bending of starlight to the birth of galaxies, from the ticking of a clock to the event horizon of a black hole — all of it is connected by one grand idea:

Space and time are not separate, but one — not static, but alive.

The universe, it seems, is a story that tells itself — written in the **curves of spacetime**, whispered through the silence of light.

CHAPTER SEVEN

Legacy of Relativity : The Unfinished Symphony

7.1 A Revolution in Thought

The story of relativity is not merely a chapter in the history of science — it is a revolution in the way humanity perceives existence itself.

Before Albert Einstein, space was seen as a silent backdrop to creation and time as the steady ticking clock that measured change. After Einstein, both became living parts of the cosmic play. He revealed that we do not move through space and time separately; we move within spacetime — a flexible, ever-changing stage that bends and stretches beneath the weight of reality itself.

Einstein's legacy extends far beyond equations. It reshaped how we imagine the universe. It turned the night sky from a distant spectacle into a living geometry, determining the fate of stars, galaxies, and time itself. It told us that the universe has a history — a beginning, and perhaps even an end — and that the same laws governing the fall of an apple govern the motion of galaxies billions of light-years away.

7.2 The Symphony of Spacetime

When Einstein gazed at his equations, he saw not just mathematics but music — a deep harmony written in the language of geometry.

"The most beautiful thing we can experience," he once said, "is the mysterious. It is the source of all true art and science."

To Einstein, the laws of nature were not arbitrary; they were compositions of cosmic music. Relativity was his symphony to that mystery — one that continues to resonate through every corner of modern physics.

The fingerprints of this theory are everywhere:

- In the ticking of GPS satellites circling Earth,
- In the redshift of galaxies racing away through expanding space,
- In the ripples of spacetime detected by LIGO,
- In the glowing ring of light captured around a black hole millions of light-years away.

Each whisper of gravitational waves, each celestial bend of starlight, repeats the same refrain: Einstein was right — and yet the story is not finished.

7.3 Where Relativity Meets the Unknown

As powerful as relativity is, it falters in the smallest realms.

In the world of quantum mechanics, uncertainty, probability, and quantum foam rule. Here, the smooth curvature of spacetime breaks down into a chaotic quantum sea — a place where even the concept of space and time begins to blur.

This is the great paradox of modern physics:

- General relativity governs the cosmic, describing galaxies, gravity, and expansion.
- Quantum mechanics governs the microscopic, describing atoms, particles, and forces.
- Each is flawless in its realm, yet they refuse to merge. Somewhere, deep in the fabric of existence, there must be a single truth to unite them — a **theory of quantum gravity.**

This was Einstein's final quest.

7.4 Einstein's Final Search

Einstein never found the grand unifying key. In the final decades of his life, he worked in solitude, searching for a mathematical bridge that could unite all of nature's forces — electromagnetism, gravity, light, and something deeper still.

The scientific world moved on to new frontiers — quantum fields, nuclear particles, modern cosmology — but Einstein remained faithful to a vision of an ordered, harmonious universe.

"God does not play dice," he famously declared — not to deny science, but to defend meaning. He could not accept that the fundamental laws of nature were written in randomness.

7.5 Seeds for the Future

Though Einstein never completed this unification, his quest became the seed for modern physics.

Today, scientists explore bold frameworks that bridge relativity and quantum mechanics —

- String theory,
- Loop quantum gravity,
- M-theory, and more.

Each of these attempts seeks to describe the tiniest threads of reality — vibrating, twisting, and weaving within the curved tapestry of spacetime. Whether these are steps toward the truth or detours along the way, they carry forward Einstein's conviction:

The universe, no matter how strange, must be comprehensible.

7.6 The Endless Spiral of Discovery

Perhaps the true power of relativity lies not just in equations but in what it reveals about us — about the human desire to understand.

Einstein's theory grew from thought experiments simple enough to imagine in a daydream:

- A train speeding along a track.
- A beam of light racing beside it.
- A man falling freely.

From such simplicity came a theory that reshaped reality. It stands as a testament to what thought, guided by curiosity and humility, can achieve.

Einstein taught us that knowledge is not a ladder climbing upward to certainty, but a spiral — circling ever deeper into mystery. Each discovery opens new questions. Each truth uncovers a larger truth behind it.

- The bending of light revealed the curvature of space.
- The curvature of space revealed the expansion of the universe.
- The expansion of the universe revealed the birth of time.
- And the cycle begins again.

7.7 The Unfinished Symphony

And so, the symphony of relativity remains unfinished — not because it lacks an ending, but because it continues to evolve.

Its melody echoes in every new detection of gravitational waves, every telescope that peers into a black hole's heart, every theory striving to unite the quantum with the cosmic. The score is still being written — note by note, by minds inspired by Einstein's vision.

In his later years, Einstein would walk the lakes near Institute for Advanced Study, lost in thought. No longer chasing equations, he sought understanding.

"I cannot believe that God plays dice with the universe. I will keep looking until I understand how the old one thinks."

He never stopped looking.

7.8 A Legacy That Reaches Across the Stars

More than a century later, humanity still looks into the depths of spacetime, into the whispers of gravitational waves, into the cosmic microwave background from the first moments of time. And in doing so, we continue walking the path Einstein began: a path of wonder, humility, and relentless curiosity.

The legacy of relativity is not merely that time bends or space curves — but that thought itself can reach across the stars.

When we look at the night sky now, we no longer see a silent void. We see the living fabric of existence, rippling with light and gravity, expanding through eternity. We see a universe both vast and intimate, ancient and newborn, mysterious yet knowable.

We see, as Einstein saw, that *reality is not a clock to be measured — it is a poem to be understood.*

And though the symphony remains unfinished, it continues to play — softly, endlessly, through every atom, every galaxy, and every mind that dares to ask *why*.

Conclusion

Einstein once transformed our understanding of the universe, but in doing so, he also transformed our understanding of ourselves. Through his vision, humanity learned that we are not observers standing outside the cosmos but participants woven into its very fabric. Every motion we make, every second we live, is shaped by the geometry of spacetime — a silent dialogue between matter and meaning. Relativity revealed that time and space are not rigid constructs but living dimensions, stretching and curving under the influence of existence itself. And in that revelation, we discovered that reality is not a static truth to be measured, but a story — one that unfolds with us, within us, and because of us.

Yet the story remains unfinished, as all great symphonies must. The echoes of Einstein's thought still ripple through the cosmos — in the faint tremor of gravitational waves, in the slow dance of galaxies, in the quiet hum of human curiosity. Each discovery adds a new note to the eternal melody of understanding. We may never hear its final chord, but perhaps that is its greatest beauty — that the universe continues to sing, and we, small yet conscious, are invited to listen. In every question we ask and every truth we seek, Einstein's vision endures — a reminder that even amid the vastness of space and the flow of time, the human mind can reach for the infinite and almost touch it.

Questioned, and understood. ***Curiosity is the first step toward discovering infinity.***